WOMEN

THE STORY OF SHE

Travis Peagler

Script Novel Publishing

Opinions Vary

In the beginning, after God created every animal of all kinds, and after Adam named everything and saw every creature had a mate, Adam searched his heart and wondered, where was his mate? Where is his delight? I imagine God heard Adam's heart quivering and smiled. God did this purposely so Adam would know what it is and how it feels to be alone... So that when he gifted him with Eve, he would never take her for granted. Men, never take your lady for granted; understand that was always God's plan, one woman for one man.

My Intent is Clear

First, you deserve a standing ovation, every woman, for simply being God's greatest gift to a man outside of salvation. Not to mention, what would life itself be without you, and I call her - she. You are mothers, sisters, friends, and Heavenly. I am a God-man, and I mean what I say. So, believe me, and many other men like me, we adore you, love you, and I mean all of you, go ahead and click repeat; you can reread it because I want to brighten your day. I want to smile, blush, and grin. We were put here to support one another, be lovers but also friends, one flesh, one twain; you can call us soul twins.

My intent is precise; I hope to unravel you with my symmetry of words called poetry. I want to entertain, uplift and feed you at the same time, word by word, line by line. Now might be a good time to grab that glass of wine. Release the stresses of your busy day and let your emotions drift away. I hope to motivate, congratulate, and touch you emotionally. I know the matters of the heart are fragile and very dear, so again, I make my intent clear. You're the reason I'm here. Sorry, I'm late. I apologize, I meant to write this some years ago, but I wasn't ready, I wasn't fully grown mentally and emotionally myself, and I knew you wouldn't want me any other way. So, here I am, and again, sorry I'm late, but I'm here now, bearing gifts of all kinds and most all - my heart, because where would we be without the firstborn of her kind that God introduced as Eve?

I hope you enjoy the poetry because it is sincerely all for you.

Contents

01

Tainted Love

Break Free

───◇◇◇◇◇◇───

I once was trapped in a cage of fear,
Where the only option was to shed a tear,
He called me names, made me feel small,
Till I was broken, I had to crawl.

But then I reached out to my kin,
And they helped me find my strength within,
My family and friends extended a hand,
And together, we came up with a plan.

I packed my bags, left behind the pain,
Turned my back on that toxic chain,
I walked away, stood up tall,
And vowed to never take another fall.

I had to break free, no longer confined,
A brand new life, a fresh state of mind,
I am strong, I am proud,
And so grateful for the support that I found.

Changing Faces

You seem to be a chameleon,
Changing colors with each new scene.
But why do you hide behind so many faces?
What are you afraid of being seen?

Is there something in your past,
That you're trying to forget?
Or do you fear rejection,
If you were to show your true set?

Whatever it is that drives you,
To put on a different facade,
I want you to know that you can trust me,
And that there's no need to feel odd.

I accept you for who you are,
Regardless of the mask you may wear.
So take off your disguise, my friend,
And know that I'll always be there.

You hide behind so many masks,
Each one a different face,
Whose identity you dare not ask,
For fear of leaving a trace.

Broken Glass

* * * * * * ◆ ◆ ◆ ◆ ◆ ◆ * * * * * *

Pieces of my past lie shattered,
Broken glass and shards scattered.
Memories once whole, now in fragments,
No glue to mend the emptiness.

Each piece, a reminder of what was,
But now just a memory lost.
The pain, the love, the joy, and the tears,
All mixed up in a jumble of fears.

I try to build anew from the bits,
But the sharp edges cut and prick.
And so I sit amongst the debris,
Picking at the pieces, until I see.

That sometimes, it's okay to leave it bare,
And embrace the emptiness, the despair.
For in letting go, we find release,
And the chance to start anew with peace.

Dare to Stay

◇◇◇◇◇◇

She was strong but scared,
Her mind and heart so conflicted.
Her love for her children weighed heavily
Against the fear that left her constricted.

He was sometimes kind, but often cruel,
His temper flaring with little provocation.
She tried to keep the peace, to soothe his rage,
To prevent another violent demonstration.

She knew her worth was more than this,
That she deserved love and respect.
But she couldn't bear the thought of breaking her family
apart, Of the pain her children would surely collect.

So she stayed, enduring the abuse,
Too much at stake, too much to lose.
She prayed for strength and for a better way out,
And guarded her heart, as her soul remained in doubt.

For though the world may judge her choice,
And question why she stayed,
She knew that she was doing what was best,
Growing stronger day by day.

And even though she lived in fear,
Her love for her children allowed her to persevere.
She chose to stay, for them, for them alone,
Until the day God bless them with a new home.

Mixed Emotions

He stands in conflict, his heart torn apart
As his feelings for her fluctuate and dart...
His mind is a battlefield, a warzone
As he struggles to figure out what he's shown.

Sometimes her touch electrifies his soul,
And the warmth of her embrace makes him whole.
The taste of her lips, the smell of her hair
Drives him wild, makes him completely aware.

But then there are times he can't take her pride
As her arrogance crushes all he's tried.
He wants to run, to escape her hold,
But something makes him stay, something bold.

He loves this woman, that's a fact,
But he hates her too, that's the impact.
Mixed emotions, that's his fate,
A never-ending cycle, an ongoing debate.

He wonders if it's all worth the pain
To love and hate again and again.
But then he remembers her smile,
And he knows he'll stick around for a while.

For in her, he has found a home,
And in her arms, he'll never be alone.
So, he'll embrace the highs and lows,
And ride the waves of love and woes.

SHROUDed PictuRE

Like changing dresses, you change faces based on the
crowded spaces.
I would say it is tasteless, but you wear the mask well...
A sweet flower, but I saw the pedals as they fell.
Many hidden drinks, but the bar well will never tell.
Perhaps that tender owes you a favor.
I'm trying to reach you so many walls around you like you built
your own jail.
Stop the facade, I know you're a living hell.
Beautifully painted face, but I see the shrouded picture behind
each pretty brush stroke.
You can lie to yourself but not to your demons.
I need you to live, and here's a list of so many reasons.
I know all your acts, but your heart deserves the Oscar.
There's a lot of love in you, don't let the alcohol consume you.

His Affair

His heart is heavy, burdened by regret
As he looks at his wife, eyes filled with sweat.
He knows he hurt her, and hurt her badly,
But his love for her is all he ever had.

He messed up, he knows, and can't take it back.
The affair has stained him, left him black.
He wants to be forgiven, wants to make it right.
But he doesn't know if he has the might.

She's hurting, and he can see the pain.
He caused it, and it's driving him insane.
He wishes he could turn back time, undo his mistake.
But he knows it's too late, his heartache is awake.

He loves her still, with every fiber of his being,
But he knows it's not enough, he's done the unseeing.
He has to face the consequences, make amend.
Hope that she'll forgive, hope that she'll be on the mend.

He'll do anything to keep his family together,
Even if it means weathering this storm forever.
His love for his wife and children will never fade,
And he'll do everything in his power to undo that betrayal shade.

Her Affair

She loved him once, with all her heart,
But then temptation tore them apart.
The thrill of a touch, the taste of a kiss
Left her wanting, addicted to this.

Her husband, unaware, still loved her true,
Unknowingly her betrayal grew.
She lied and she sneaked, she lived a lie,
While he worked hard to provide.

Now the truth is out, the damage is done;
She's ashamed of what she's become.
She's sorry and guilty, she's in a mess;
But with all her heart, she wants to confess.

She knows she messed up, badly so,
But she still loves him, that he should know.
She hopes and prays he'll understand,
And somehow forgive her wandering hand.

The memory haunts her every day,
Of what she did, of what she took away.
She longs for the love she shared before,
But she's stained and tainted forever more.

Drowning Love

—— ◇◇◇◇◇◇◇ ——

The thirst was too much to quench, wanting more than just a sip.

I demanded cups of it until my chin and chest were stained with it.

Since a girl I yearned for it more than anything,
I hadn't been drinking love but was being poured cups of
effectuation.

I rushed patience to speed up the fairytale.
Now, my emotions are in chains, and my heart is in jail.

I saw it eluded many around me, and I was determined to catch it.

I overshot my shot, and failed to understand it ... the love story of
poverty, damn, I missed it.

A gift that was free, but I choked the hell out of it, abused and
mistreated it, honestly, because I feared it.

My beautiful body is my magnet, but my soul is so ugly... So how
could love ever want me?

Mendacious Love

Your body's mine, your heart's not there,
Your mind's elsewhere, empty and bare.
Every night, I lead you astray,
But your soul still keeps me at bay.

God tells you I'm not who I seem,
But you submit to my every scheme.
I reign over your sensual pain,
But your trust in me is in vain.

You pray to be released from my hold,
But your body's mine to have and to hold.
Our love's a lie, a game we play,
But you can't resist my wicked way.

As the night fades and morning comes,
You leave me and walk back to your old chums.
But I'll be waiting for you to come back,
For our mendacious love is our only track.
I love the sweet and sour melody of infidelity as the hook plays
out... Your favorite part of the song, and we're both past grown.

So dance with me in this sweet deceit,
Our love's nothing, but a poetic conceit.
Your heart and soul are mine to steal,
For in this mendacious love, is how you like to feel.

When Doves Don't Cry

We were two ships in a stormy sea,
Tossed and turned by every wave we see.
Our love was like a sandcastle in the tide,
Washed away, no matter how we tried.

We fought and argued, tears shed in vain
Trying to make something work that was too stained.
Every day was a battle, every night a war.
We couldn't fix what was broken before.

We held on tight, hoping for the best,
But eventually, we had to give it a rest.
Our once sweet love had turned into pain.
Our hearts no longer beat the same refrain.

Now, we're just strangers passing by.
Our love story, just a distant lie.
We tried to mend, but it was all in vain.
Our love was a thunderstorm, not a summer rain.

Baptized With Lies

He says he loves you, but is it true,
When he only romances when it's convenient to do.
Leaving you when you need him most,
Leaving you feeling like a forgotten ghost.

Sincerity in his eyes so bright,
But his tongue drips with deceitful spite,
Lies that leave you feeling lost and confused,
Words that break your heart and leave you bruised.

Is this all that love is meant to be,
A fleeting moment of romance and glee?
Or can it be something deeper and true,
A bond that lasts when the skies turn blue?

So, take a step back and really see,
Is this love or just a fantasy?
Don't let his words blind you from the truth,
For love should be sincere and rooted in proof.

Burn Out

We loved so hard, we loved so true,
That no one else mattered but me and you.
We laughed, we danced, we shared our dreams
Till the world became hazy and nothing was as it seemed.

Our love burned so brightly, it blinded the sun.
We were two hearts fused together as one,
But the flame grew too hot, we lost control.
And before we knew it, we were both consumed whole.

Our madness grew bigger with each passing day,
Till our love had become something I could never say.
It twisted and turned, it became something dark,
And suddenly, I found myself in a loveless park.

You had become someone I didn't know:
A stranger wearing the face of love, that I couldn't show.

The love story was gone, our love had turned mad,
And it left behind a heart that was broken and sad.

So, I walked away, I left you behind.
From you, I had to escape what once was kind.
But even though it's over, my heart will find love again.

Sleeping With The Enemy

Hey love ... You look unhappy, so unfulfilled. I see a beautiful slave tied to his side. You wish to leave but fear of loneliness grips you… So terrifying of all the ones that came before you.

If I could, I would take you from him. I turn strong hands into soft hands for you, something that man could never understand.

Do you know how I feel for you? Feeling rapid pulsations of your beating heart, trapped behind enemy lines while unwillingly sleeping next to the enemy.

Trust is not easy, I know, but this I know ... I love you ... Does he? I know your worth, I see your beauty and inner power. If I could, only if I could, I would.

Words of Fade

Your voice, a symphony of deceit,
Whispers sweetly, my heart to beat,
But hidden within the tomb of your love,
Lies darkness, cold as the shadows above.

Your dominance, a trap that I cannot escape,
Prominence that suffocates, a cruel fate,
You speak falsehoods, but I long to believe,
That every word you say, I can trust and receive.

But now I see through your mask of lies,
The truth revealed, and my heart dies,
For every promise made was just a fade,
An illusion, a mirage, a masquerade.

So, now I must leave you behind,
No longer will I be blind,
To the fiction that you speak,
My heart, too precious, to treat so meek.

So, farewell, my love, and goodbye,
I'll spread my wings, and learn to fly,
Away from the catacombs of your embrace,
To a life of truth, and a love that won't erase.

Winter Days

I wish to give all my winter days away. You can have them, please take them, do what thy will, if you wish you can throw them away.

No need to pray about this decision, I have buried all my dead relationships there, none of them shall rise.

Treasonous if any believes this because my tongue is a lie. The hurt and pain, the pain and the hurt, my heart no longer beats, but beeps, can you hear the difference?

I've been programmed, so now I'm different. I'm not indifferent to how they feel about me. I'm to blame for it all, I've always been heartless, pointing at flawed parents they're the ones who taught this,

I was old enough to know and still decided to buy this. I'm flawed too, I thought this was my only gift to give to all the ones that loved me. Winter days I gave yes, I know until Jesus took them away.

Tainted Love
◇◇◇◇◇◇◇

Pieces of me, fragments of she, we're both broken,
deafening words no longer heard when spoken.

Romance sparked off lies that became true...
One night ran into another, ok, so now every day I'm feeling
you.

We see the door but no one leaves...
Just like rent, we know love ain't free.

In your eyes, you wanna flee kidding yourself, love, I see heart
bleeds for me...

So, I'll keep on taming, why you keep on praying.
I do my job well, the wet sheets tell the tale.

Deep down, that's what you want the most but it's not what
you need. Just like a vampire, that kitty has to feed.

So tainted, true indeed, but we understand each other and
sometimes that's all one needs.

02

Flesh Tales

Guilty as Sin

Guilty pleasures, oh how sweet,
They offer solace and retreat.
But in the end, they lead to pain,
A nightmare we cannot contain.

The need for sex, so strong and raw,
It drives us forward without flaw.
But when we give in to its call,
We often find ourselves in thrall.

For what we seek is only flesh,
A momentary thrill at best.
But it leaves us feeling empty,
Like we've lost our inner plenty.

The darkness that these pleasures bring,
Is more than just a fleeting thing.
It creeps into our minds and hearts,
Tearing us apart.

So, let us be aware and wise,
Of the dangers these desires disguise.
Let us seek true love and light,
And banish darkness from our sight.

Arouse Me, and I, You

Not the typical man trusting he only can keep what's held in his hand. Seeing is not always believing, love. But teach me, love, show more than your exterior galore. Arouse me, feed my mental, I need to believe you hold hidden gems yet to be explored. See... your body will always heat me, but only your mind can keep me. A woman's true sexy is in her thoughts. See... That right there can never be bottled, sold, or bought. You deserve your throne, many of the xy-chromosomes have never learned. But I see you, I mean I really see you. I can see you as far back as when God crafted you from Adam's rib... I know your worth and the history of your birth. So, don't sell yourself, cheap love, you are worth more than gold love. So, arouse me, and I, you.

Within Her

For in the secret place, the endless paradise awaits,
the gift of all gifts that has enticed men for centuries without
end forever baits.

In the secret place so peaceful and fair,
Lies the endless paradise beyond compare.
It's a gift that's been coveted through the ages,
A journey that turns hearts into pages.

The journey once taken, transforms all within,
An experience that's rare, not just a whimsical whim.
It changes our thoughts and alters our,
It opens our eyes and leaves it all behind.

The endless paradise is a place of peace,
A realm where our worries and burdens all cease.
It's a place of love and joy and grace,
A home where our faith has its perfect space.

In this secret place, we find the gift of all gifts,
A treasure that's priceless beyond what money uplifts. It's the
journey of a lifetime that will forever remain, An adventure
that will never be the same.

Bleeding Heart

Let your heart bleed free... You can trust me. When I love, I love so true, even if you scare me. I've never met another on my level. The Bible says that when we fully connect, we will be one flesh, one twain. All I've ever wanted was for you to be mine. Once while I was thinking of you, I saw your reflection over mine... As I gazed in the mirror, I felt that this must be a sign. Or is it just me in a delusional state of mind because I want you so much, wanting more from you than just physical touch?
I want your heart. I want your mind. I want all of you. I promise to love and kiss all your flaws once I find. I am with you all the way, on bended knee, will you marry me?

Gifted lips and fingertips. When I touch you, you'll know, I'm the only man that can unlock the depths of your soul. Wise old tales be told but what's the truth in it? Truth is when I find love, I put my foot in it. Meaning I'm all in, more ways than one. I want to romance you, just like I'm slow dancing you.

My delicate rosemary flower, sometimes, I just want to make love to you and others I wish to devour... Passion strokes so strong have you reaching for a higher power.

Let's be clear we are spiritual beings, so when I say I'll have you reaching, that's what I mean.

Let Go of passion and bliss, our bodies intertwined as we kiss.

No more insecurities or hesitation, for in this moment, we have found love and elation.

Continued...

Let's explore each other's bodies, learn what makes us feel alive. With each touch and caress, our love will thrive.

Nothing can hold us back now, for we have found our match. Let's make love until the morning light, our bodies in perfect catch.

A virgin no more, but a queen in my eyes. Let's continue this journey together, as we watch our love rise.

So, let's dance, my love, and never let go. For in your arms is where I know, the world is right and our love will forever grow.

Let Me Take You

Our fingers intertwined, our hearts beating fast,
As we stroll under the moonlit sky, tonight will last.
I'll trace your lips with mine, and make you feel alive,
Our passion ignites, as we get lost in each other's eyes.

I'll whisper sweet nothings, and make you laugh,
My arms around you, protecting you from any rough path.
We'll dance under the stars, and sing our hearts out loud,
As long as we're together, nothing will bring us down.

I'll cherish every moment, every touch, every kiss,
Our love will only grow, as we share this bliss.
Let's hold hands maybe, and kiss you, baby,
Our love, an eternal flame, burning ever so crazy.

Te'azane

Te'azane, charmer of women,
His heart a vessel of lust,
A prisoner of his own making,
Trapped in a cycle of love and dust.

Each night a new nectar,
Each kiss a fleeting pleasure,
But with every conquest,
He felt emptier and emptier.

For many sex slaves cannot fill the void,
Of love and genuine connection,
And so he danced on,
A lost soul in constant reflection of damnation.

Oh, Te'azane, you handsome rogue,
An unwitting victim of desire,
He's tired of playing games and getting too close to the fire.

Tired of being a male predator and pleasing the dark shadows
that hid in his room, waiting to consume him. But he knew
the name of Jesus and shouted it out loud, been married for
almost twenty years now, and is a proud father.

Wanted Dead or Alive

The collector of hearts, a predator he was,
Devouring love, leaving women a lost cause.
His harsh disdain, a weapon he wielded well,
Taking hearts, leaving behind a loveless hell.

Who was this man, sent to wreck such destruction?
A gift or a curse, his actions a vile obstruction.
Who taught him this behavior, what drove him to such depravity?
His birth mother, a monster, or the twisted hand of fate's
irregularity.

The collector of hearts, a hollow man at best,
Left only the shattered remains of those whose love he would test.
But in the end, what fate awaits the empty-handed thief?
A life of isolation, with no love or solace, only misery and grief.

So, beware the collector of hearts, and keep your love guarded well,
For he will come, in the guise of love, your heart to quell.
But with steadfast resolve and a heart free of fear,
You can resist his charms, and keep your love safe and dear.

Mistakes Made in The Night

In the heat of the moment,
The flesh takes control,
Ignoring all reason,
Convinced it knows the goal.

One-night stands are the ticket,
To satisfy the urge,
But the morning after,
Brings waves of regret and purge.

The body feels empty,
The mind consumed by guilt,
The heart wishes for something more,
A bond that won't wilt.

It's a mistake to learn from,
A momentary pleasure,
But it's important to remember,
Love is the real treasure.

The flesh wants what it wants,
But it's the soul we need to please.

Lust Had to Die

A slave to temptations that I could not hide.
Lust, like venom, coursed through my veins,
Binding me tighter with its relentless chains.

But in the midst of my struggle, I found solace anew,
For I turned to the One who is eternally true.
In God's embrace, I sought a guiding light,
To lead me through the shadows of my darkest night.

With every breath, I begged for renewal,
To be cleansed of impurity, to find spiritual fuel.
And in His infinite grace, I found a way,
To shed the shackles and begin a brand-new day.

As time passed by, I witnessed the transformation,
The evil within me started to lose its foundation.
The rust of sin crumbled, getting weaker with time,
For His love and mercy had started to climb.

God's healing touch mended my battered soul,
His blessings poured over me, making me whole.
In His word, I found teachings so profound,
Guiding my steps on this holy ground.

With patience as His virtue, He taught me to love,
To cast aside false desires and rise above.
In His gentle arms, I exhaled the shadows of despair,
And embraced a newfound love that was immensely rare.

Continued...

Yet, through this journey, I know the struggle still lies,
For demons try to seduce, their whispers fueled by lies.
But with God as my shield, and faith as my sword,
I'll stand tall in His strength, trusting in my Lord.

So, let me testify, in all honesty,
That in God's love, I found my destiny.
Though flaws remain, and battles might ensue,
I surrender to His mercy, His love pure and true.

03

Serenity's Kiss

Forever Love

They met when they were young and free,
In a world so vast and full of possibility.
They fell in love and vowed to be,
Together for all eternity.

Through the years they faced many a trial,
Their love, though, never lost its power to rec-
oncile.
Together they overcame life's setbacks,
With faith and love their bond never cracks.

Through seasons of joy and sorrow,
They knew their love would still not borrow.
From paths of anger or pain,
For they knew the beauty of love to gain.

As the years marched on, they grew old and frail,
But their love was as strong as ever, it never failed.
They continued to laugh, live, and love,
Guarding their bond from any push and shove.

They showed us that true love never rusts,
But only grows stronger, with time and trust.
Now, with wrinkled hands and hearts beating as
one,
They look back on their journey, and all the
joys they've won.

Love is Here

This love is like no other,
It fills me up like no other lover.
He's passed each and every test,
Proving his love is true, no less.

I never thought that I'd be blessed,
With someone who's good, and true to the test.
A year later, and he's still around,
I'm afraid to believe, can this be the true love I've found?

His love is patient, kind, and sincere,
He wipes away my every tear.
He holds me close, and never let's go,
With him, my heart has found its home.

I've never known such love before,
It's deeper than anything, and so much more.
I'm afraid to embrace it fully, you see,
For the fear of losing him completely.

But I will be brave, and take that chance,
And fully embrace this romance.
For when true love comes your way,
You have to grab it, and let it stay.

So, here's to the best love I've ever had,
The one who's made my life less sad.
I'll hold him tight, and never let go,
For with him, my heart will forever glow.

The Beauty of Women

Oh women, you are truly divine,
With your grace and beauty so refined.
Your smile can light up the darkest of days,
And your touch can heal in so many ways.

From the moment of birth, you are endowed,
With magic that seems to astound.
You nourish your young with love and care,
And teach them to grow, to learn, to dare.

You are the nurturer, the giver of life,
The one who stands strong in times of strife.
Your heart is a haven, a sanctuary of peace,
Where we find solace, love, and release.

Your beauty is the world's first perfume,
A fragrance that lifts us out of gloom.
Your eyes shine bright like the stars above,
And your touch fills us with warmth and love.

So, here's to you, dear women of the world,
Your worth and value can never be unfurled.
You are God's greatest gift, a blessing so true,
And we thank and appreciate all that you do.

Glitter in the sky, you love,
A love that shines so bright,
A love that fills my heart and soul,
And makes everything feel right.

With every moment that we share,
I feel the warmth of our love,
A love that's pure and true and deep,
Sent to us from up above.

From the first time I saw you,
I knew that you were the one,
The one who would light up my world,
And bring all my dreams to come.

Together we walk hand in hand,
Through life's journey, side by side,
With love as our guiding star,
We face whatever may arise.

Glitter in the sky, you love,
With each passing day, I know,
Our love will only grow stronger,
For together, we continue to grow.

And so I give my heart to you,
To cherish and hold and treasure,
For in your love, I find my strength,
And my heart fills with joy and pleasure.

Beautiful

━━━◇◇◇◇◇◇◇━━━

You are the essence of beauty,
The strength of generations past.
A daughter of the earth,
A jewel that will forever last.

You were lost in the darkness,
But now you have been found.
A queen within your own right,
With a throne to astound.

You are a part of me,
A reflection of my soul.
Together we rule the world,
And make each other whole.

I bow to you, you kneel to me,
Together we set each other free.

So, wear your crown with pride,
And let your light shine bright.
For you are more than a woman,
You are a source of pure delight.

The seed of Eve, mother earth,
A goddess in her own right.
May your heart forever beat strong,
And your spirit burn ever bright.

Imperfect Maybe

She once looked in the mirror,
With critical eyes so sharp,
Her curves and flaws she'd scrutinize,
And feelings in her heart.

The world told her how to be,
How to look and what to wear,
She'd try to mold her body,
Trying all means fair.

But one day, she looked closer,
And saw a new image appear,
A woman with flaws and curves,
Who was simply being sincere.

She no longer saw the stretch marks,
Or blemishes on her skin,
She looked beyond those qualities,
To what was deep within.
She saw strength and beauty there,
And a woman who was proud,
To simply be herself at last,
Her heart shouted out loud.

Her body wasn't perfect,
But her beauty was unique,
There was no one else like her,
No matter how she'd seek.

Continued...

She stood proud in front of the mirror,
Embracing her real self,
Knowing that perfection was a myth,
And self-love meant good health.

So, if you see this woman now,
You'll see a different view,
No longer holding on to the world's ideals,
Just being herself, true blue.
Imperfect maybe, but perfect for me, I'm that lady.

Life is tough, that's for sure,
And it's easy to get lost in the allure
Of giving up and settling for less,
But that's not what life should be, I confess.

We've only got one shot at this game,
And it's up to us to stake our claim.
So, don't let fear hold you back,
Stay the course, stay on track.

Follow your dreams, chase your bliss,
Don't let anyone tell you what you miss.
You're the one in control of your destiny,
So, create the life you want, be free.

It won't be easy, that's no lie,
But if you keep pushing, you'll reach the sky.
And when you look back on your life one day,
You'll be proud of the steps you took to find your way.

So, don't waste your time on what could have been,
Instead, break free and begin again.
Follow your dreams, live your life,
Embrace the adventure, overcome the strife.

Overcome

Self-doubt, pain, and regret,
A trinity of agony we can't forget.
Moments of weakness, times of despair,
Can trap us in a cycle that's hard to bear.

But there's a light that can be found,
A way to lift our feet off the ground.
We must remind ourselves of this truth,
That we are stronger than our youth.

The pain we feel is just a phase,
It's a cloud that will slowly fade.
The suffering too will draw to a close,
And what remains are lessons we can boast.

Regrets are footprints of the past,
But we can make this moment last.
Use our experiences as a guide,
And never let them lead us astride.

So, hold your head up high my friend,
And let your doubts and fears transcend.
For you have the power deep within,
To overcome and begin again.

Anxiety Who

When worry and fear consume my heart,
I turn to God to do my part.
He calms my anxious thoughts and fears,
And wipes away my streaming tears.

Though storms may come and winds may blow,
In His arms, I find my peace and flow.
His love is my anchor in the midst of the storm,
And in His strength, my fears transform.

He reminds me that I am not alone,
And in His presence, I have a home.
He comforts me with His gentle voice,
And surrounds me with His endless grace and rejoice.

With each breath, I feel Him near,
And in His presence, I have no fear.
For with Him, I can conquer all,
And my fears will no longer enthrall.

Her Power

· · · · ◆ ◆ ◆ ◆ ◆ ◆ ◆ ◆ ◆ ◆ ◆ · · · ·

She stands tall, with head held high,
A symbol of strength, she does not shy.
She faces challenges, big and small,
And always stands firm, through it all.

She does not need a man to lead,
For she is strong enough to take the lead.
She fights for what she believes,
And never gives up, or concedes.

Her voice is strong, her words are true,
And she speaks for those who can't speak too.
She stands up for rights and equality,
And won't back down from any authority.

Through trials and struggles, she never falters,
For her resilience is something that can't be altered.
She knows her worth, and it shines through,
A true powerhouse, this woman in view.

She is the epitome of grace and might,
A beacon of hope, shining bright.
And though adversity may come her way,
She'll always be strong, come what may.

Daily Grind

I have goals, dreams that I want to achieve,
But poverty seems to keep me from what I believe.
Paying rent, bills, and necessities take a toll,
The future seems bleak without some role.

I work hard each day, hoping to save
To break free from this economic grave,
But money is tight, and expenses rise.
I fear to stay here, my aspirations demise.

I wonder if others face similar strife
Of being career-focused and living a poor life.
The battle to balance ambition and survival
Is a challenge that demands many revivals.

I cling to hope, despite the despair
That poverty's chains are not forever there.
With some luck, hard effort, and a break,
I'll break free from this cycle and make.

Thus, I struggle with the daily grind
Keeping my head high, striving to survive.

I Slay

She worked hard day and night
To make a better life
For her children and herself
No matter the struggle or strife.

She was determined and strong,
Never giving up her dreams.
She climbed higher and longer
Than it sometimes seemed.

She chased her career
As if it were her only chance
To give her family the future
They deserved in advance.

With each promotion and raise,
She felt a sense of pride
Knowing she was making a difference
In her children's lives.

She taught them to work hard,
And strive for something more
To never give up or settle
For anything less than what they're worth.

And through her words and deeds,
She proved that anything's possible
If you put your mind to it
And are willing to be responsible.

Continued...

She proved that a woman
Can have it all in life
With hard work, faith, and love.
Anything can be sacrificed

So, here's to the career-focused woman
Who lives life on her own terms.

Boss World Lady, you're a force to be reckoned with,
With a spirit that's fierce and a heart full of grit.
You've climbed the ladder and paved your own path,
In a world where women too often get left in the past.

You've earned your right to play this game
on your own terms, To set your own goals,
and watch your dreams burn. With
each step you take, you inspire those
around, empowering others to wear their
own crown.
You call your own shots and play by your own rules,
With a confidence and grace that is truly cool.
You've faced challenges head-on,
and conquered them all, Your unwavering
strength is something we all
should applaud.

So, here's to you, Boss World Lady, and all that
you've achieved, Your success is a reminder of what can be. May
you continue to grow and reach new heights, A true inspiration,
and a shining light.

Love Letters

In these love letters, he pours out his soul,
His adoration for you, he can't control.
Each word, a testament to his devotion,
And a reminder of your love potion.
With every note, your heart is renewed,
The weight of the world lifted, and love ensues.
The worries of life fade away,
As you read his love letters day by day.
Life may be unpredictable and fleeting,
But love is a constant, always worth keeping.
So, let his love letters be a reminder,
To cherish each moment, in love's splendor.
Live with passion, love with your whole heart,
Find joy in each moment, never to be apart.
Together you'll weather life's highs and lows,
With his love letters to keep you close.

Candy Snow

· · · · · ◆ ◆ ◆ ◆ ◆ ◆ ◆ ◆ ◆ · · · ·

In the land of Candy Snow,
Where the sweetest love does grow,
We dance and twirl in the wind,
With true love that will never rescind.

You enchant me with your love,

So, pure and holy like a dove,
My heart beats fast with joy,
My mind full of thoughts that employ.

Together we spin and spin,
Dizzy from love that's within,
At this moment, we are free,
To love each other endlessly.

Oh, love me through the end,
With you, my heart will always bend,
Blowing together in the wind,
Our love will never rescind.

Enthralling love that we share,
In the land of Candy Snow so fair,
With you, I'm lost in ecstasy,
Forever in love, you and me.

If You Love Me Pay Me

Equal pay for every woman,
It's not just a dream,
It's a fundamental right,
That we should all esteem.

Our work is just as valuable,
As anyone else's you see,
So why is it that men,
Always seem to make more money?

It's a simple concept,
And yet it's hard to grasp,
That just because we're women,
Our salaries are not the last.

We work just as hard,
And often times even more,
But when it comes to pay,
We're shown the lesser door.

So, let's stand up for ourselves,
And demand what we are due,
Equal pay for every woman,
Is a battle worth pushing through.

*W*omen

With a great melody intertwined with a heavenly body. Short or tall big or small. From chocolate covered to vanilla smothered. With the gift of song that releases your soft sweet voice giving all men no choice but to rejoice. Like a beautiful sight to watch a dove gliding away from the water's shore with a touch from you, that is so pure. With a scent that yells romantic, with the taste of chemistry that produces organic juices, the temptress of the universe crafted with great delicacy from the tip of your nose to the middle of your bones that connects your spirit to your soul with the eyes being the window revealing all that she has to tell to give another your love is a gift of the one that awaits you in the mist, recited by mouth, pressed by the pen; this praise can only come from a man.

Soul Mates

Soul mates we were
Before we were sent off and before the earth was formed...
We had eyes and a heart but no shape or form. Clasped
together before time was time and before clocks ticked... But
still, we knew why we were created and what love meant.
Our spirits were sent down to earth. You in the shape of a
woman, me in the shape of a man... The Heavenly Father
wiped out our memories of each other with His mysterious
ways we were not meant to understand; Set free from our
purity no longer being guided by His hand... His intentions
were not to put us to a test but on a quest, to see if we
could find each other as strangers and return to Him as
Angels.

Tech love...

—— ◇◇◇◇◇◇ ——

An unexpected connection
Born from a simple online interaction
Conversations that grew in intensity,
But it was more than just a virtual affinity.
So much common ground,
A shared sense of humor, we found
Not just about looks but about our beliefs:
A connection that gave our spirits relief.
Through messages and chats,
We discovered emotions like love and compassion
Building a bond that lasted;
We realized tech love will never be outdated.
We laughed and shared our dreams,
Our hopes and aspirations, it seems
In each other's presence, we found solace;
Our love, though virtual, was flawless.
It might have started online, but it blossomed into something
real,
An unexpected love that we could truly feel,
Tech love, a bond that's pure and true;
Just like any other love, it's life-changing too.

Conversations

I enjoy our conversations,
A safe space for contemplation.
Your words always strike a chord,
A connection that can't be ignored.

We share dreams and aspirations,
Challenges and life lessons.
It's amazing how much we relate
Like we're meant to communicate.

But we're both married, so we know
That exploring would be a mistake to go.
But I'm grateful for this friendship we've built;
It's a treasure that can't be bought or rebuilt.

Our conversations may not lead to love,
But our connection is a gift from above.
I cherish our talks and your kind heart;
Let's continue to strengthen this bond and never drift apart.

Make it Rain

· · · · ◆ ◆ ◆ ◆ ◆ ◆ ◆ ◆ · · · ·

As a man, I stand tall and proud
Demanding justice to be allowed
For every woman who has been downtrodden
For every salary that's been ungodly sodden.

It's about time we level the playing field,
Giving every woman what they truly wield.
It's a matter of human dignity, not gender
For every pound of work, they should earn one just
as tender.

It's not enough to pay lip service to equality,
We must take action and end this atrocity,
For too long, women have been paid pennies on the pound,
While men in similar roles have been profusely crowned.

Let's break this vicious cycle of gender pay gap,
And stop the disregard for every woman's map.
Their skills are worth just as much as any man's,
And it's about time we woke up to the plans.

We must fight the patriarchy with all our might,
And let every woman know that they have the right,
To demand the wage that they are worth,
And eradicate gender discrimination from this earth.

A Celebration

As you grace the room with your presence,
My heart swells with admiration and reverence,
For you, my dear, are a celebration,
Of all that's stunning in this earthly creation.

Your beauty is unmatched, a work of art,
A symphony in motion, every move apart,
Of a dance that mesmerizes, a beauty so divine,
That it could make the stars above, simply shine.

And then there's your intellect, sharp and bright,
A mind that could unravel the mysteries of night,
Or bring to life a world so new and bold,
As to captivate every heart, young and old.

Your walk, oh how can I ever forget,
So sexy, so confident, so full of zest.
It's a marvel to behold, a sheer delight,
As to make every head turn, every eye bright.

So, here's to you, my dear, a celebration indeed,
Of all that's lovely, all that's brilliant, all that we need.
May your radiance shine, bright and true,
And light up this world, with all that's beautiful and new.

Fire Starter

You are the sun that shines so bright,
The only one who brings me light.
For you, I'll walk a thousand miles,
Cross oceans, climb the highest peaks, and conquer trials.

I'll shoot across the stars,
Leave behind Venus and Mars.
I'll set the galaxy ablaze,
Just to have you in my embrace.

I'll steal the colors of the rainbow,
Drain the seas where the deep fish glow.
I'll journey to the end of the earth,
To experience the beauty of your worth.

For you, I'd scorch a thousand suns,
Pollute every moon, and carry on.
I'll do anything to have you near,
And cherish you, my love, forever dear.

Love

Love is both kind and cruel, both tender and rough,
An enigma that no science can contain,
A story woven into the fabric of life's stuff,
A song whose lyrics are danced in lovers' refrain.
It is an art that masters never quite achieve,
A ploy that poets endlessly attempt to define,
A gift that many give and yet many receive,
A brand that burns forever in the lovers' line.
Love is a flame that neither flickers nor dies,
A seed that grows and blooms with time's gentle care,
A power that's unveiled by gazing into each other's eyes, A
passion that transcends the if and the where.
It is, in essence, the essence of life itself,
The beauty of existence in its purest flow, A dance to where the
heart leads, free from worldly wealth,
A journey whose end we can never truly know.
Love is a conundrum, a puzzle to be solved,
A mystery unwrapping before our eyes,
A mix of emotions that cannot be resolved,
A journey through highs and lows that surprise.

Beyond what we can see,

There lies a world so vast;
A universe of mystery,
Where the future and the past
Collide and intermingle,
Where anything can be.

Beyond what we can see,
There lies a world unseen;
A place where magic beckons,
And dreams become routine.
A land of untold wonders,
Where anything can be.

Beyond what we can see,
There lies a world of sound;
A cosmic symphony,
where harmony is found
In every note and rhythm,
Where anything can be.

Beyond what we can see,
There lies a world of thought;
A realm of boundless imagination,
Where ideas can be wrought
Into art and science,
Where anything can be.

Patience

In this waiting game, we learn to trust
Our hearts are open, but our minds adjust
To the pace of life and the timing of fate
As we seek to find love and escape the waiting state.

Patience is key, we know this to be true.
We must surrender control and let our hearts renew
The course of our lives, the paths we take.
We trust in God's plan and the love He will make.

Our hearts may ache, our passions may rise,
But we hold our ground and stay true to our goodbyes.
For we know that patience yields the sweetest fruit,
And in time, true love will take root.

So, while we wait, we nurture our souls;
We heal our wounds and set our goals.
With faith and hope, we navigate the tide
Guided by love, we let patience be our guide.

Patience is a virtue we must embrace,
As we navigate this uncertain race.
Waiting on God to guide our way,
To lead us towards a brighter day.

Farewell

Farewell, my dear, it's time to part;
Our journey together must come to a start.
I hope you find joy and love in your life;
May your days be filled with happiness and lights.

It's hard to leave, but it's for the best,
Our paths may cross again, but for now, I'll rest.
Take care, my friend, I'll always cherish our time.
Goodbye for now, may your spirit shine. Goodbye is hard to say,
But it's time to walk away.
No more words need to be spoken,
Our ties now are broken.

Wishing you nothing but the best,
As I lay this chapter to rest.
Life goes on, and so shall we,
May happiness forever be.

Expressions

With every hue you choose,
You express your love or blues.
Soft strokes of pink for affection,
Or dark blotches of black for rejection.

Your canvas comes alive,
With splashes of blue, green, or thrive.
Each stroke tells a story,
Of your joys and woes, vivid and gory.

Your paintbrush dances on my wall,
Capturing emotions that make you tall.
Be it fear, anger, or elation,
Your art is a reflection of your emotion.

In my home, your feelings find a place,
A canvas where they can embrace.
And I am grateful for this art,
That lets me see your soul's every part.

So, keep painting your feelings true,
For my wall is a canvas meant for you.
And every time I behold your art,
I feel blessed to be a part.

God Made

Man and woman, God made,
Together they're meant to be laid.
Nothing can come in between,
True love is forever to be seen.

Every human being, created by a divine hand
Man and woman, equal in strength and grand
No claim of gender, if it's not biologic
Respect and honor, is the right logic.

No confusion or distortion of what is pure
God-made sexes, sacred and secure
No society or individual can change this
Principles of life, can't go amiss.

So, let's not deceive ourselves, in this age,
Let's appreciate our differences, let's engage
Man and woman, to complement each other,
A divine plan, to cherish forever.

In this truth, let's stand and abide,
No matter the trends, no matter the tide,
God's creation is beautiful and divine;
Let's honor it, till the end of time.

Cheers to You

Cheers to you, my dear, for standing strong,
For being who you are without a single wrong.
Your beauty, grace, and strength, shine;
You're a masterpiece of the divine.
Cheers to you, for embracing your flaws,
For being bold and tearing down all walls.
You're a warrior, fierce and true;
A force to be reckoned with, through and through.
Cheers to you, for loving yourself,
For being unapologetic and never needing help.
You're a beacon of hope for all to see;
A reminder that all can be free.
So, cheers to you, my lovely friend,
For being yourself until the very end.
May your light continue to shine so bright,
And may you always remain a woman, day and night.

Will You

You are the rhythm of my beating heart,
The melody that soothes my soul,
You are the lyrics to my favorite love song,
The one that I never want to grow old.

Every note you sing, every word you say,
Is like music to my ears,
You are the sweetest melody,
A symphony that erases my fears.

Your love unchains the depths of my heart,
Bringing out emotions so pure,
You are the inspiration for my art,
A muse, an angel, so true and so sure.

I cherish each moment we spend together,
And treasure every memory we make,
My favorite love song will be forever,
The one composed of the love we take.

On bended knee, I come to thee,
With love and devotion, my heart's decree.
The depths of my soul are known only to thee,
But this I know, my love will forever be.

Through sunshine and storm, I'll stand by your side,
With gentle touches and words that won't hide.
My love will lift you up, it will not chide,
For this I promise, my heart will never subside.

Continued...

On bended knee, I plead with thee,
To take this ring and my heart, and forever be with me. My love
will bless and enrich thee,
For this I ask, will you marry me?

I Trust You

Oh Lord, my heart is heavy with pain,
My body aches, my mind is drained.
I cry out to You, in need of Your grace,
To heal my wounds, to restore my faith.

It is Your will, that I know
To trust in You, and not let go,
For You are the healer of all things,
The source of life, the King of kings!

I surrender all, to Your loving hands:
My fears, my doubts, my life's demands.
You know me better than I know myself,
And Your love for me is greater than my health.

So, I cling to You, with all my might,
For You are my hope, my strength, my light.
I declare that my healing is on its way,
For in You, there is the power to change today.

Thank You Lord, for the gift of life,
For Your faithfulness, and sacrifice.
I trust in You, and Your perfect will,
To heal my body, and to make me whole again.

What is Love

Love is not a thing that you can buy,
No matter how much money you try.
It's not a commodity to acquire,
Or a bargain that you can admire.

Love is a feeling that comes from the heart,
And it cannot be measured or torn apart.
It is not a game that is played for fun,
Or a temporary fling that can easily be undone.

Love requires your commitment and trust,
Built on a foundation that is strong and just.
It asks for your honesty and dedication,
And a willingness to make sacrifices for its preservation.

So, if you want to experience true love,
Understand that it's a gift from above.
And to obtain it, there is a simple fee,
Your unwavering commitment and honesty.

A Friend or Shadow

Friends come and go, or do they,
If they quickly shift like wheat, then who dey?
For shadows love to dwell and tell your secrets,
A friend would fight until the very end to keep it.

You, my dear, a grown-tass woman, strong and bold, years
past five years old, No need for pretend friends, whose true
intentions will scold. In the realm of friendships, it's quality
we seek, Not mere numbers, but souls who truly speak.

Seek those who stand by you, through highs and lows,
Through laughter and tears, when the darkness grows.
For in their loyal presence, you'll find solace and cheer, A
resolute connection that soothes all fear.

So, shed the pretenders, those who come and go, Embrace
the genuine, the ones who truly know, That a grown-tass
woman needs friends who remain, Through life's trials and
triumphs, hand in hand, in this insane game.

For true friends are not formed overnight,
But through shared experiences, tested by life.
They lift you up when you falter and fall,
And celebrate your victories, big or small.

A Mother's Crest

You are a mother, a natural nurturer,
Life is in your hands, the most sacred treasure.
You guide with love, you heal with care,
You comfort with words, you're always there.
Your heart is pure, your soul is kind,
Your warmth surrounds, your touch so divine.
You sacrifice your all, for your child to thrive,
You protect with all your might, with every breath
you strive.
A mother's love is unconditional,
It knows no bounds, it's never optional.
You are the light in your child's dark,
You are the hope that guides with the brightest spark
Your love is the foundation, the rock that stands,
For every child to walk, to run, to take a chance.
You are the mother, the role model to follow,
Your love is the greatest gift, a foundation to
build tomorrow.
Thank you, dear mother, for all that you do,
Your heart is full of love, your soul is true.

His Ways

In the midst of chaos and strife,
We need to find our inner life;
A place of peace, calm, and still,
Where we can rest and recharge our will.

The world may be in turmoil and pain,
But we can choose to break the chain,
To focus on the good and the light,
And let our spirits take flight.

God's ways may seem mysterious and strange,
But we can learn to trust and engage
With the love and grace that surrounds us,
And find the peace that will ground us.

So, take a moment to calm your soul,
And let the healing power take control,
Breathe in deeply and exhale slowly,
Let the peace inside you grow wholly.

For in this stillness and serenity,
We can find the strength and the clarity to stop the bleeding,
To face the challenges that life may bring,
And to soar on the wings of Heaven's tea.

Go

In this world of competition and struggle,
It's easy to let go and just juggle
Between a routine that's mundane and dull,
And an ambition that's exciting and full.

But if you want to soar high and fly,
You've got to fight and give it a try.
Don't wait for destiny to come your way,
Make your own fate, make it happen yesterday.

The longer you wait, the more you get trapped
In a nine-to-five job that leaves you tapped. So, take a step
forward, take a leap of faith,
And chase your dreams with unwavering faith.

You may stumble and fall, you may face defeat,
But it's all part of the journey, a learning seat.
Keep pushing forward, keep giving it your all,
And watch as your dreams and aspirations sprawl.

So, don't wait for tomorrow's excuses, they show up on the
psyche like asphyxiation bruises.
It's your destiny and testimony that awaits your future. If you
can imagine that, your heart will indeed clap.

Here and Now

I can't wait, I need your love today, your heart continues to sway, I want to embrace it.

But I can't chase it, if you let it beat free, let it choose where it wants be.

Promises may never be fulfilled and time never yields, but tomorrow may never come for me.

I'm here now in the flesh, praying to God for that man, and here he stands, and now, you are speechless?

True love only comes in waves of three, claim it now or leave it be.

True Love

True love is a feast, a delightful affair,
With courses aplenty, beyond compare.
An appetizer of laughter, light and sweet,
Setting the tone for the love we will meet.

Two sides offer balance, like yin and yang,
Supportive and caring, a lifelong pang.
One brings strength, the other brings grace,
Together, they form a perfect embrace.

And like a fine wine, love must be chilled,
Allowing our hearts to be slowly filled.
With warmth and affection, it will enhance,
Every moment we share, every loving glance.

But before we savor each bite and each sip,
We must close our eyes and let our hearts skip.
We'll ask God for blessings, for love that will last,
Through every challenge, present and past.

For true love endures the valleys of life, lions, tigers, and bears, oh
my. Through struggles and hardships, through joy and strife.
And as the years fade, the gray turns to white,
Our love will only grow stronger, shining more light.

So, let us treasure this love we have found,
Nurturing it gently, on solid ground.
With gratitude and faith, we'll walk this path,
Hand in hand, navigating love's aftermath.

Continued...

Together, we'll create a lifetime of bliss,
Sealing our love with every tender kiss.
For true love, like a full-course meal that's truly satisfying...
morning, day, and night.

Live Free

I pray that you live a life so bright,
That your light shines on through the darkest night,
That you leave a mark in hearts you've touched,
And memories that'll never be lost.

So, go ahead and live your best life,
Chase your dreams, conquer your strife.
For in living, you inspire us all
To stand tall and answer our own call.

Live with your heart in the open,
With the wind in your hair.
Live with your spirit unbroken,
With a strength rare.

Live with the fire in your eyes,
With a passion that never dies.
Live with a soul that never lies,
With the love that forever flies.

Live with your dreams held tight,
With the courage to take flight.
Live with your spirit alight,
With the joy that's pure and bright.

Live every moment with grace,
With a smile on your face.
Live free and unafraid,
With a heart that's unbetrayed.

Transcendence

In the realm of eternal skies,
Our love shall forever rise.
For it is a flame that won't subside,
A connection that can never hide.

Oh, dear beloved, how I believe,
That true love, God would never leave.
For He bestowed upon us this bliss,
A love so sublime, impossible to dismiss.

Though circumstances may tear us apart,
In my heart, you'll forever be a part.
A love renewed, a love reborn,
Beyond the realms where mortals mourn.

In the embrace of heavenly grace,
Our souls shall find a divine space.
A love untamed, like stars that gleam,
In a celestial dance, a cherished dream.

I shall forever adore you, my dear,
Through joys and sorrows, near or afar.
With unwavering love and boundless support,
In my heart, our connection will transport.

Though fate might twist and intervene,
Our love will shine, ever serene.
For in the essence of eternity's flow,
Our souls entwined, forever to grow.

Continued ...

So, let us embrace this earthly love,
And pray for blessings from above.
For in this world or the next, we'll claim,
A love's transcendent, forever the same.

Lucidity

In the boundless book of my existence, I offer
up every page,
With unwavering honesty, my vulnerabilities I
engage.
No hidden chapters, no secrets to conceal,
For in revealing my truth, the intimacy we can feel.
Each line tells a tale of joy and woe,
The highs that paint my dreams, the lows that
weigh me low.
From youthful adventures under the vibrant sun,
To battles fought, battles won, and wars yet to
come.
Through tender verses, I lay bare my soul,
Imprinting memories, both sweet and bitter,
making me whole.
Every anecdote, a stepping stone to growth,
A symphony of experiences, my life's oath.
There are moments of laughter, where smiles
abound.

Through shared mirth, sacred connections are
found.
But shadows linger too, in the corners of my
heart,
Places of longing that yearn for a fresh start.
I offer you this tale, with love, sincerity, and
grace,
For your eyes, the mirror that reflects my face.
In your understanding, my story finds meaning,

Continued...

And in your embrace, I find my ending, gleaming.
Let this tale be etched within our hearts,
forever bound,
As we dance in the closure, a har
mony profound.
For you, my confidant, my destiny intertwines,
In your embrace, my story finds its divine.
So, take these pages, hold them tenderly,
Together, we'll author a beautiful ending.

Where Was God

In the depths of despair, where darkness does confound,
Where life's cruel blows make hope seem to drown,
When pain overtakes and tears stain your eyes,
You gasp for breath, believing it's your demise.

But in that moment, when all seems lost,
When despair and anguish are the heavy cost,
The angels above begin to weep,
As God touches you gently, your soul He does keep.

For where was God when life was unkind,
When you longed for solace, but none could you find?
He was there in the shadows, holding your hand,
Whispering softly, "This too shall withstand."

When friends turned their backs and walked away, When
loneliness lingered like an unwelcome stray,
God stood by your side, never wavering or shy,
Offering solace, His love never runs dry.

For God knew your pain, He saw every tear,
He felt every heartache, every unspoken fear,
In the depths of your sorrow, He remained truthful,
Declaring the devil's lies, revealing them as futile.

So, do not despair, for God still cares,
Even when life's burdens become too much to bear,
He remains your solace, your guiding light,
In the darkest of days, He'll make everything right.

Continued...

For when life beats you down, beneath the ground,
When breath seems lost, and death does surround,
Remember, dear friend, with a hopeful sigh,
God is there, always, saying, "The devil is a lie."

God Validated You: No Likes Needed

In the realm of life and creation's embrace,
A masterpiece emerged, adorned with grace.
A vessel of strength, love, and divine light,
A being meant to shine, illuminating the night.

God's creation, so wondrous and true,
Designed uniquely, with purpose imbued.
Not for the sake of man's mere delight,
But to bring forth harmony, love, and ignite.

You don't need a man to validate your worth,
For your value transcends the bounds of this earth.
God saw the void and crafted you with care,
To be a source of love and joy, beyond compare.

In your soul, resides a sacred fire,
A power that lifts spirits higher and higher.
For God knew man needed your light to thrive,
In your presence, the world comes alive.

You were chosen to radiate love's pure essence,
To bring compassion, strength, and resilience.
To stand tall, embrace the power within,
Knowing that validation comes from God, only from Him.

So, do not seek worldly approval, dear soul,
For God's love and embrace make you whole.

Continued...

You are enough, cherished, and complete,
Covered by God's love, eternally sweet.

Remember, true love, you are beautifully made,
With a purpose in this world, to never fade.
Your validation lies beyond Earth's facade,
For it comes from the Creator, the everlasting God.

About the Author

Travis Peagler is an accomplished and acclaimed author who has earned recognition for his exceptional work, with a captivating storytelling style and his script novel series. He delves into various genres to create books that engage and inspire readers. Whether it's teaching valuable lessons, uplifting spirits, offering escapism, or sparking wonder, Peagler's stories have a profound impact.

Peagler demonstrates exceptional versatility as a writer, mastering multiple genres and proving that no subject matter is beyond his capabilities. With his passion for storytelling, he is able to seamlessly navigate between different styles and themes, ensuring that his readers are consistently entertained and intrigued.

His dedication to the craft of writing is evident in the numerous titles he has published. Through his extensive body of work, Peagler has proven himself to be a prolific author committed to delivering engaging narratives. His contributions to the literary world have garnered him numerous accolades and awards, further solidifying his status as a respected and talented author.

www.TravisPeagler.com

Acknowledgments

Dancing like nobody was watching, our eyes met, and I couldn't look away. At that moment, I knew I had found something special that had been hidden from me.

Our love story began with spontaneity, breaking the norms, and embracing the unexpected. We defied expectations and followed our hearts, not knowing where this journey would lead us. But we trusted in God's guidance, believing that He had a purpose for bringing us together.

Through the ups and downs, the joys and the sorrows, we learned the true meaning of partnership. We faced challenges that tested our commitment, but through it all, we held on tight to each other, relying on our faith to guide us.

We've built a life together, creating a home filled with love, laughter, and endless memories. From the adventures we've shared to the quiet moments of intimacy, every experience has deepened our connection.

You have been my constant support, my rock in times of uncertainty. Your unwavering belief in me has pushed me to strive for greatness and become my best version. You have seen me at my lowest, yet you never stopped believing in the strength within me.

And together, we have grown. We have learned the importance of forgiveness, patience, and compromise. Our love has weathered storms but has only grown more robust and more resilient.

As we celebrate nearly twenty years of marriage, I am reminded of the countless blessings we have received. Our children, who are a testament to our love, bring immeasurable joy into our lives. They are the legacy of our commitment and the embodiment of our love.

To my dearest wife Stacey, I am forever grateful for every moment we have shared. You have been my source of inspiration, my partner in crime, and my best friend. Together, we have built a bright love that shines bright, illuminating our lives, those around us, and our forever night.

I look forward to the next chapter of our journey, and to the adventures that await us. With you by my side, I know that we can conquer anything that comes our way. Thank you for being my everything, my soulmate, and for choosing to spend this extraordinary life with me. Here's to many more years of love, laughter, and happiness. I love you, now and always.

www.ingramcontent.com/pod-product-compliance
Lightning Source LLC
Chambersburg PA
CBHW071212120626
46546CB00006B/2529